TWIN CITY TRACTOR
PHOTO ARCHIVE

TWIN CITY TRACTOR
PHOTO ARCHIVE

Photographs from the
Minneapolis-Moline Company Records

Edited with introduction by
P. A. Letourneau

Iconografix
Photo Archive Series

Iconografix
P.O. Box 18433
Minneapolis, Minnesota 55418 USA

Library of Congress Card Number 93-79372

ISBN 1-882256-06-9

93 94 95 96 97 98 99 5 4 3 2 1

Cover and book design by Lou Gordon, Osceola, Wisconsin
Digital imaging by Pixelperfect, Madison, Wisconsin

Printed in the United States of America

PREFACE

The histories of machines and mechanical gadgets are contained in the books, journals, correspondence and personal papers stored in libraries and archives throughout the world. Written in tens of languages, covering thousands of subjects, the stories are recorded in millions of words.

Words are powerful. Yet, the impact of a single image, a photograph or an illustration, often relates more than dozens of pages of text. Fortunately, many of the libraries and archives that house the words also preserve the images.

In the Photo Archive Series, Iconografix reproduces photographs and illustrations selected from public and private collections. The images are chosen to tell a story...to capture the character of their subject. Reproduced as found, they are accompanied by the captions made available by the archive.

The Iconografix Photo Archive Series is dedicated to young and old alike, the enthusiast, the collector and anyone who, like us, is fascinated by "things" mechanical.

ACKNOWLEDGMENTS

The majority of photographs which appear in this book are part of the Minneapolis-Moline Company Records, and were made available by the Minnesota Historical Society. We are most grateful to the society, and sincerely appreciate the cooperation of its staff. Supplemental photographs were provided by the editor.

INTRODUCTION

In March 1903, Minneapolis Steel & Machinery Company (MS&M) was formed to fabricate steel for buildings, bridges, flour mills, and similar structures. The company also established a small foundry and mechanical department. Soon after its founding, MS&M began manufacture of Corliss steam engines, which were sold to mill and grain elevator operators under the Twin City name.

In May 1904, management concluded that the emerging market for gasoline engines offered the company a better opportunity for profit. In June, they sent an engineer to Europe to investigate potential designs and, by October, MS&M had secured rights to build gasoline engines, under license from G. Luther and Company, Braunscheig, Germany. By mid-1905, a prototype was tested and, in early 1907, the company sold its first 2-cylinder stationary unit.

After three years, the engine operations had not turned a profit. Determined to establish MS&M as a viable gasoline engine manufacturer, the directors decided that a vertical, 4-cylinder 7 x 10-inch engine should be developed and fitted to a traction chassis. In February 1910, MS&M signed a contract with Joy-Wilson Company to develop five tractors, from a design completed by McVicker Engineering Company. The first two machines were built in February 1911 and were sold in South America, after which the company committed to build 200 to 250 of a redesigned tractor, the Twin City 40, for the 1912 season.

The Twin City 40 or 40-65 was built until 1924. The tractor, tested at Nebraska in August 1920, featured a 4-cylinder 7.25 x 9-inch engine, rated at 535 rpm. The test unit produced 49.71 maximum drawbar horsepower and 10,820 lbs drawbar pull. The tractor weighed 25,500 lbs. Its transmission offered a top forward and reverse speed of 1.9 mph.

From 1913 to 1920, MS&M offered the Twin City 60-90. Originally rated at 110 engine and 60 drawbar horsepower, it featured a 6-cylinder vertical engine with bore and stroke of 7.25 x 9-inches. Weighing 28,000 lbs, this behemoth was equipped with a 116 gallon capacity cooling system and a 95 gallon fuel tank.

In 1913, the company also introduced the Twin City 25-45. Basically, a smaller version of the TC-40, it featured a vertical, 4-cylinder 6.25 x 8-inch engine, and weighed 16,000 lbs. Production ended in 1920.

Between 1913 and 1917, MS&M built the Twin City 15. The TC-15 was originally fitted with a transversely mounted engine. Later tractors carried a parallel mounted, vertical, 4-cylinder 4.75 x 7-inch engine, rated at 650 rpm.

In 1917, MS&M introduced the sleek Twin City 16, the first Twin City tractor with fully enclosed gears. Perhaps best described as a light heavyweight, its 4-cylinder 5 x 7.5-inch engine was rated at 30 engine and 16 drawbar horsepower. Its transmission offered two forward speeds of 2 and 2.25 mph. Production of the 16-30 was suspended in 1920.

The industry's move away from heavyweight tractors to smaller, more maneuverable machines dates to about 1913. MS&M's entry into the lightweight market was somewhat delayed, however, due to its relationship as a contract manufacturer for the Bull Tractor Company. Between 1913 and 1917, MS&M built the immensely successful but short-lived Little Bull. The agreement between the two companies precluded MS&M from building its own competitive small tractor for one year beyond the termination of their relationship. By 1919, MS&M introduced the first of its own true lightweights, the Twin City 12-20. The 12-20 engine featured a unique 4-cylinder, sixteen valve design, with two intake and two exhaust valves per cylinder. Rated at 1,000 rpm, the June 1920 Nebraska test unit recorded maximum 18.43 engine and 27.93 drawbar horsepower. The 12-20 fea-

tured unit frame design and a transmission with two forward speeds of 2.2 and 2.9 mph.

In 1927, the 12-20 was re-rated and designated the Twin City 17-28 or Model TY. In its Nebraska test of May 1926, the 17-28's engine featured 4.25 x 6-inch bore and stroke. The test unit developed maximum 30.91 engine and 22.5 drawbar horsepower, with drawbar pull of 3,777 lbs. The tractor weighed 5,895 lbs, as tested. The Twin City 17-28 remained in production until 1934, by which time Minneapolis Steel & Machinery had merged with Moline Implement Company and Minneapolis Threshing Machine Company to form Minneapolis-Moline Power Implement Company.

In 1919, MS&M also introduced the Twin City 20-35. Built along the lines of the 12-20, it featured a larger 5.5 x 6.75-inch 4-cyliner engine. In October 1920, it was tested at Nebraska. The test unit recorded maximum 46.88 engine and 34.12 drawbar horsepower, with drawbar pull of 5,730 lbs. The 20-35 weighed 8,100 lbs, as tested.

The 20-35 was later re-designated the Twin City 27-44 or Model AT. In May 1926 at Nebraska, it developed maximum 49.05 engine horsepower and 5,640 lbs drawbar pull. The test unit weighed 10,500 lbs. Both the 20-35 and 27-44 offered a 2-speed transmission. As with the 17-28, the 27-44 remained in production beyond the merger that created Minneapolis-Moline.

In 1929, prior to the merger, MS&M introduced the Twin City 21-32 or Model FT. A standard tread tractor, it featured a 3-speed transmission and a vertical, 4.5 x 6-inch 4-cylinder engine. Weighing 6,189 lbs, the 21-32 developed maximum 5,092 lbs drawbar pull. Production of the 21-32 ceased in 1932.

Also introduced in 1929 and built until 1934, the Twin City KT or Kombination Tractor featured a high-clearance standard front axle, which permitted its use as both a cultivating and plowing tractor. Its 4-cylinder, 4.25 x 5-inch vertical engine was rated at 23 engine and 14 drawbar horsepower. The KT featured a 3-speed transmission and optional power take-off. The tractor was redesignated the KT-A in 1934 and remained in production until 1938.

While Minneapolis Steel & Machinery survived the depression of 1920-21 and, in fact, prospered in the last half of the 1920s, competition among tractor manufacturers proved fierce as the decade closed. International Harvester regained its position from Fordson as the dominant tractor manufacturer; Case, Allis-Chalmers and Massey-Harris expanded to become full line suppliers; and John Deere added a general purpose tractor to complete its line. By 1928, it became obvious to MS&M management that the company could not survive on its short line of tractors and threshing machines. Knowing that both Moline Implement Company and Minneapolis Threshing Machine Company were for sale, the suggestion was made that a new company be formed amalgamating the assets of all three companies. In April 1929, MS&M sold its assets to Minneapolis-Moline Power Implement Company, bringing its 27 year history to a close. The new company continued manufacture of the Twin City line of tractors, eventually dropping the Twin City name in favor of that of Minneapolis-Moline.

A few of Minneapolis Steel & Machinery Company workers. *(Bureau of Engraving, Minneapolis)*

A view of the MS&M factory facilities.

MECHANICAL DRAWING ROOR

Wednesday noon meeting of factory workers.

A CORNER IN THE MACHINE SHOP

FOUNDRY

CENTER BAY OF MACHINE SHOP

18

Tractor assembly area.

Twin City 12-20 tractors in storage. January 1920.

1918 Minnesota State Fair exhibit.

23

TWIN CITY 15

Twin City Model 15-30.

Twin City Model 15 with late style radiator.

Twin City Model 15 with early style tubular radiator.

TWIN CITY 25

Studio photographs of a Twin City 25.

Ten ton road roller based on TC-25.

Twin City 25.

Twin City 25 with tracks. California. 1915.

Twin City 25 pulling a 12-foot Adams grader, as it builds a reservoir for oil producers to store salt water. Texas. September 1917.

Twin City Model 25 pulling wagons.

TWIN CITY 40

Right and left hand views of a Twin City 40.

Right hand view of a Twin City 40. *(Bureau of Engraving, Minneapolis)*

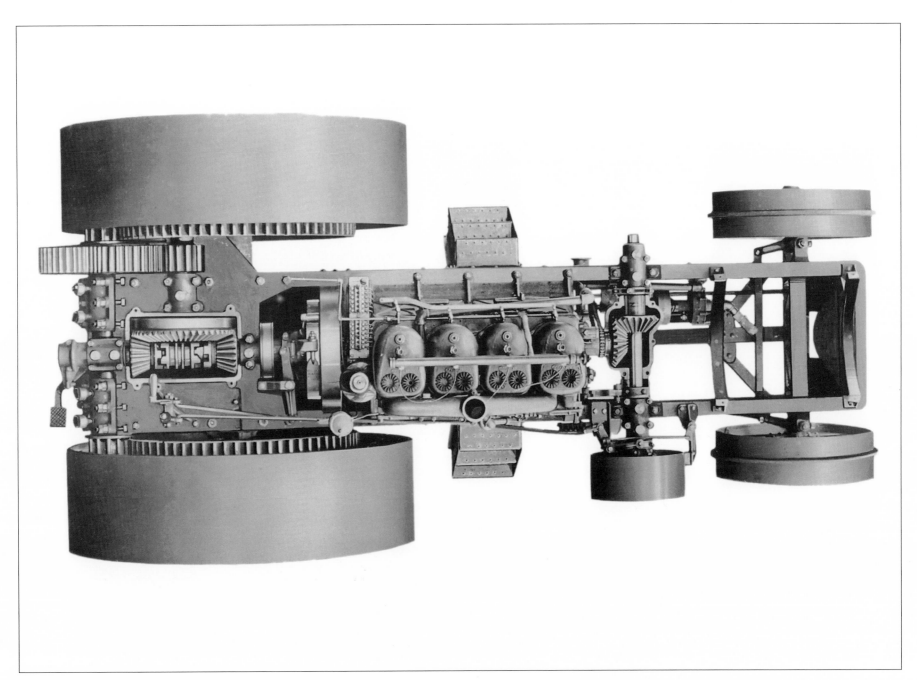

Overhead view of the TC-40 chassis. *(Bureau of Engraving, Minneapolis)*

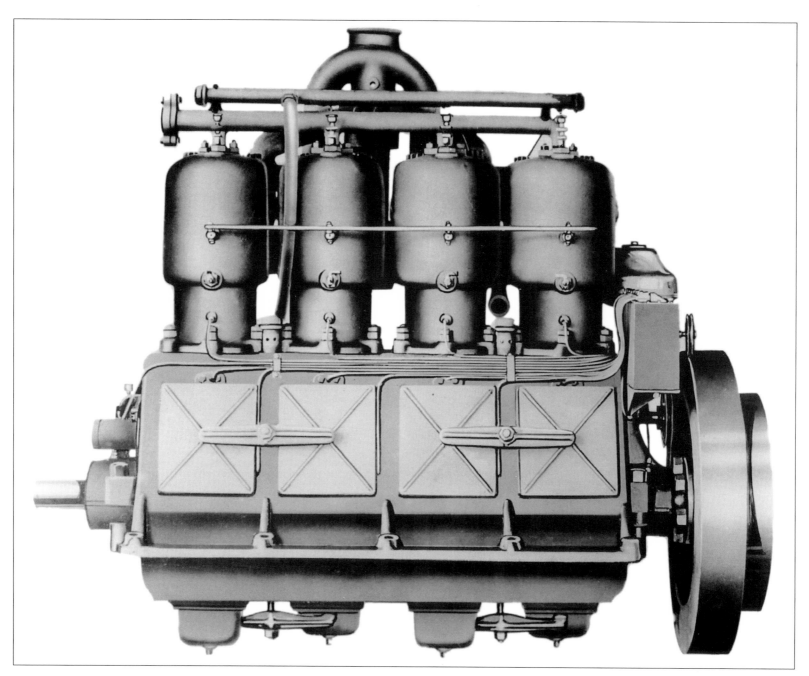

Twin City 40 engine. *(Bureau of Engraving, Minneapolis)*

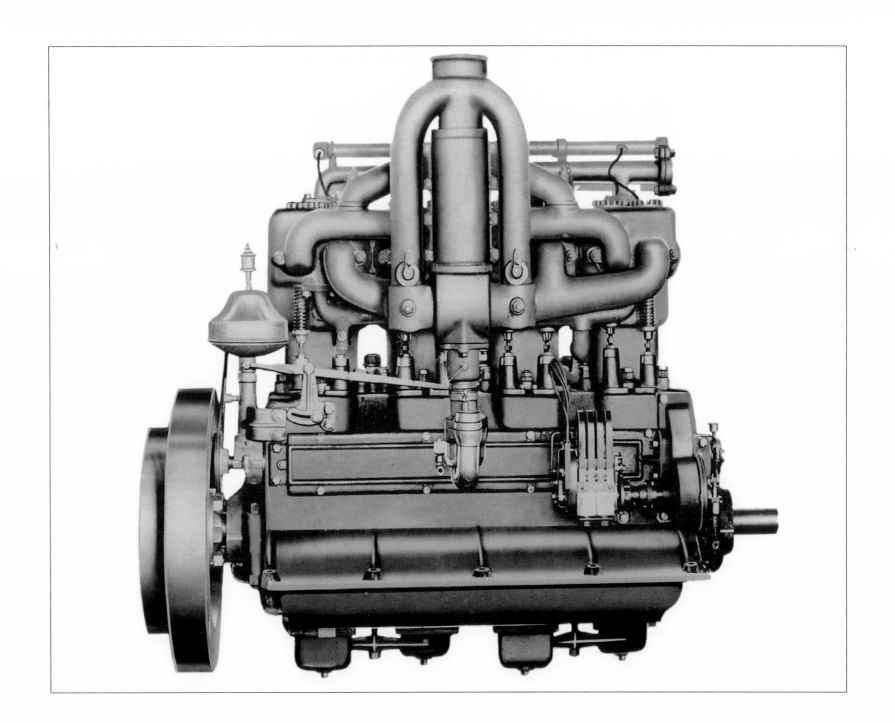

Sectional view of Twin City 40 engine, from wash drawing.

44

Right hand view of TC-40.

Twin City 40 cutting wheat. Dalton, Nebraska. February 1918.

Threshing with a TC-40 on the 22,000 acre Dalarymple Farm near Casselton, North Dakota.

TWIN CITY 60

TC-60 left hand view.

TC-60 right hand view. *(Bureau of Engraving, Minneapolis)*

TC-60 left hand view. *(Bureau of Engraving, Minneapolis)*

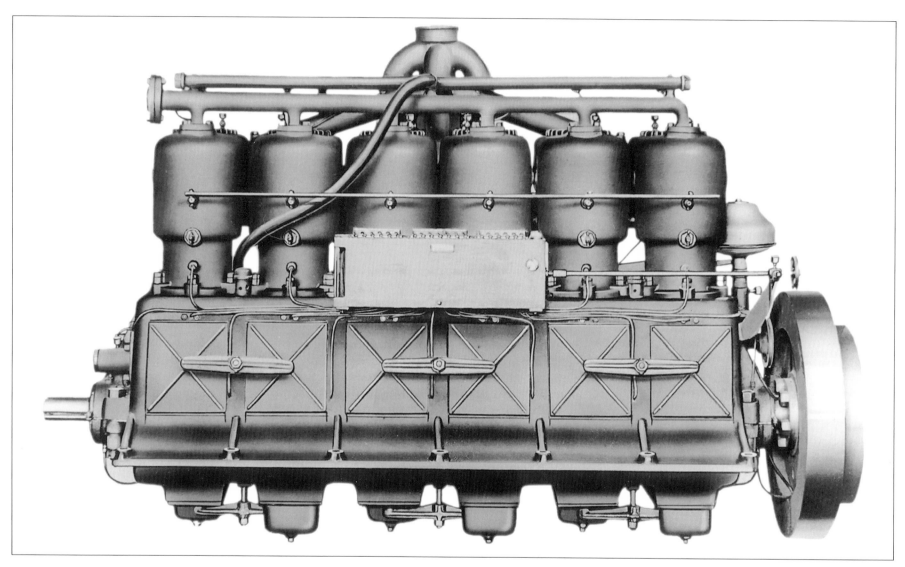

Twin City 60 engine. *(Bureau of Engraving, Minneapolis)*

TC-60 owned by General Contracting Company, Minneapolis, at work on Osseo Road. July 1918.

TWIN CITY 16

Right hand view of Twin City 16-30. 1919. *(Bureau of Engraving, Minneapolis)*

Close-up of driving compartment. Photograph taken for Model 16-30 instruction book. June 1919.

TC-16 wheel and dust guard.

TC-16 pulling Russell grader. California. Circa 1919. (Bureau of Engraving, Minneapolis)

TC-16 operating thresher.

TWIN CITY 12-20

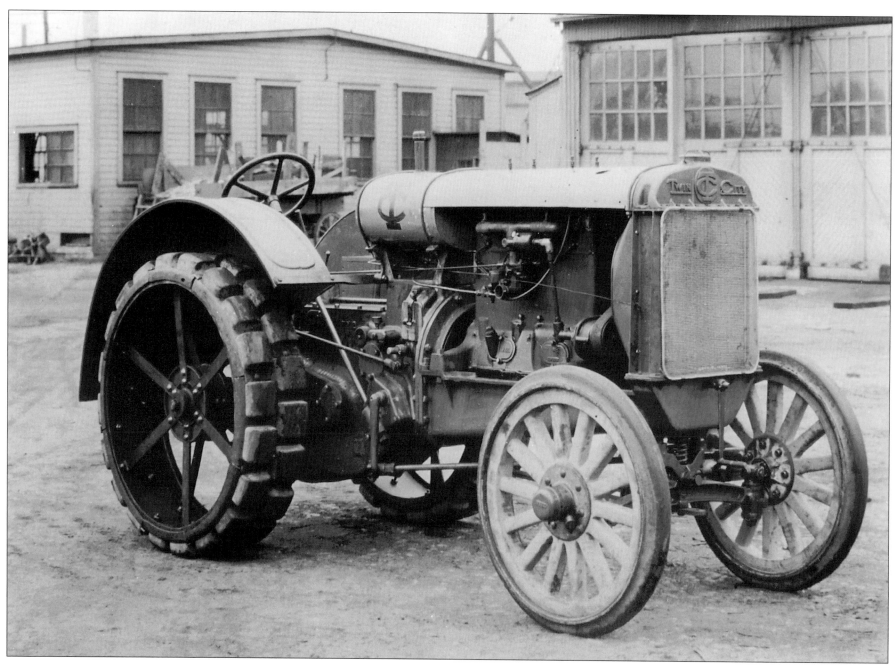

Twin City 12-20 industrial tractor.

Twin City 12-20 orchard tractor with citrus fenders.

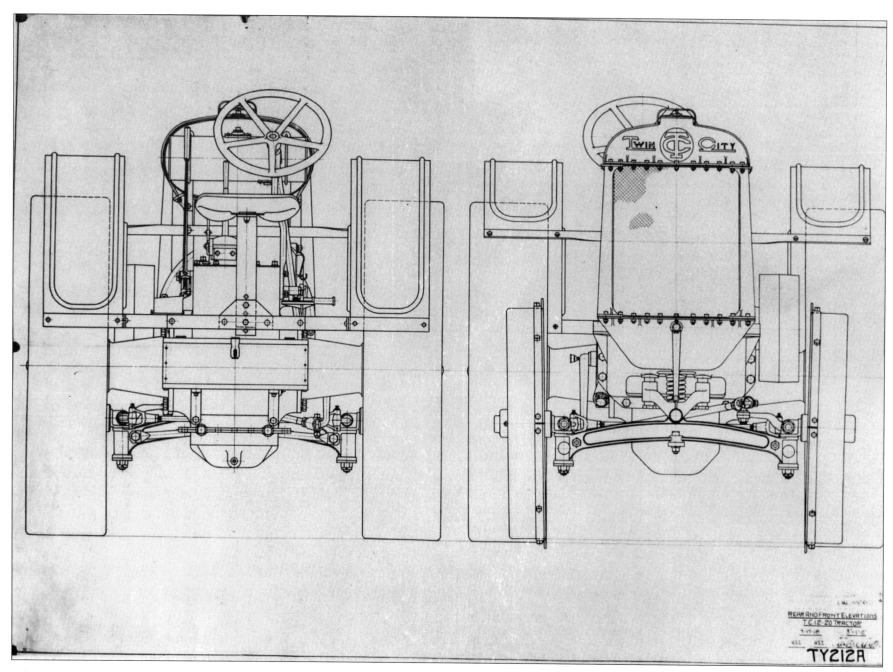

Blueprint of Twin City 12-20 front and rear views.

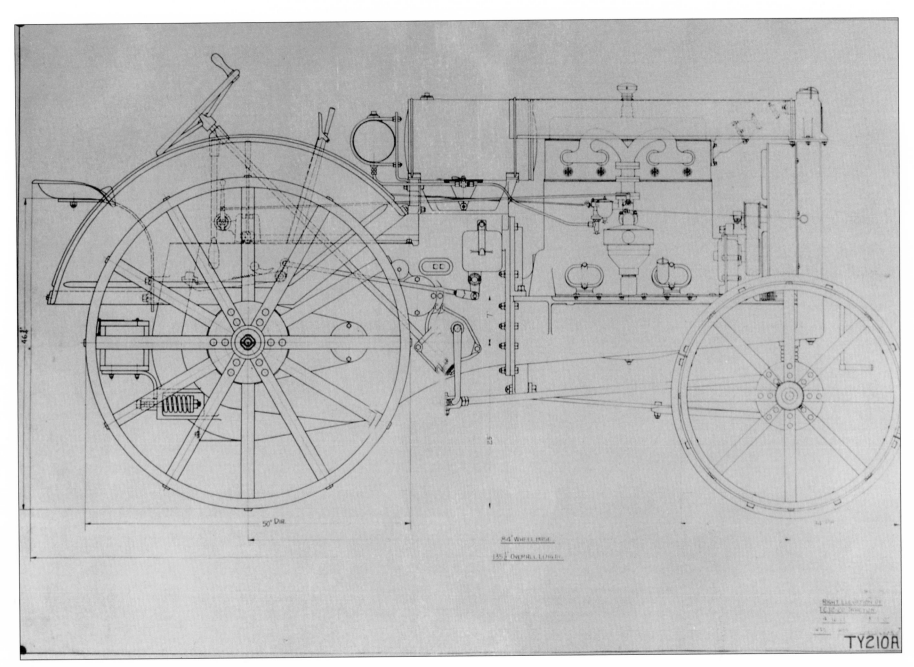

Blueprint of Twin City 12-20 side view.

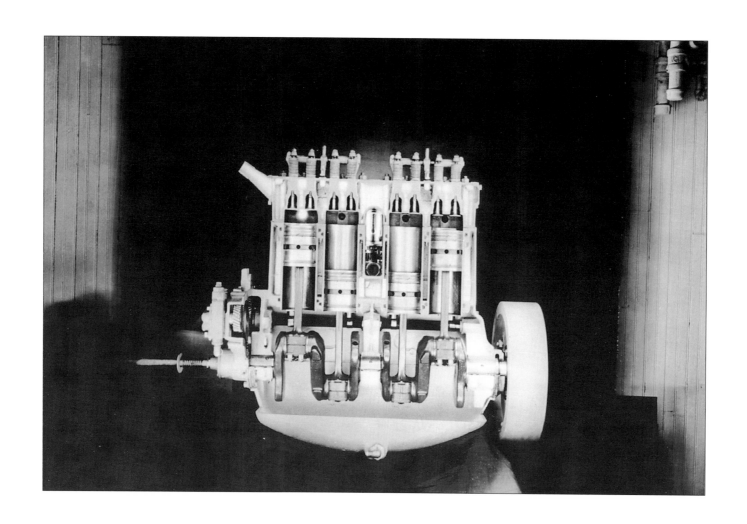

68

Three views of the Twin City 12-20.

Unloaded and photo taken Dec. 28-26
for A.O. Espe - Crookston - Minn

70

TC 12-20 clearing trees for a golf course. South St. Paul, Minnesota. June 1920.

TC 12-20 plowing with 3-bottom Oliver plow. October 1918.

TC 12-20 plowing. April 1920.

Back view of 12-20 in alfalfa field.

76

Twin City 12-20 with 4-disk plow near Fargo, North Dakota. November 1919.

Twin City 12-20 pulling disk and drill. July 1920.

TC 12-20 and binder ready for the field.

TC 12-20 pulling corn harvester.

Rear view of TC 12-20 pulling new ensilage cutter. October 1920.

TC 12-20 pulling two 8-foot binders with shocker attachments.

12-20 and thresher.

TC 12-20 hauling corn. January 1920.

Grader based on Twin City 12-20. *(Macks Photography, Waterloo)*

Rear view of TC 12-20 grading roads. September 1920.

TC 12-20 with road maintainer.

TC 12-20 with road maintainer.

Grading roads in Minneapolis. November 1919.

Twin City 12-20 plowing snow. Minneapolis, Minnesota.

Side view of TC 12-20 equipped with rubber tires. March 1921.

TWIN CITY 17-28

Three-quarter left view of Twin City 17-28.

Front view of TC 17-28.

TC 17-28 disking. McCook, Nebraska. *(Ellington Studio)*

Two TC 17-28s and thresher.

Twin City 17-28 and Adams Road Maintainer.

TC 17-28 and plow.

Rear view of TC 17-28 with 4-bottom plow.

January 1928 Cleveland Road Show. *(H. Koss)*

TWIN CITY 21-32

Twin City 21-32.

TC 21-32 with cab.

TC 21-32 and plow.

Twin City 21-32 with roll-over plow. 1928.

TC 21-32 with hay wagons.

TC 21-32 and thresher.

Industrial version of TC 21-32. *(Bureau of Engraving, Minneapolis)*

Twin City 21-32 with Galion 14-foot blade. Fairfield, Nebraska. *(Nepho)*

TWIN CITY 27-44

Twin City 27-44.

TC 27-44 pulling three 10-foot disks.

Twin City 27-44 demonstration.

TWIN CITY KT

Model KT tractor on display. (Larson Photo)

Twin City KT.

Three-quarter right front view of Twin City KT.

KT with integral cultivator.

KT and plow.

Twin City KTI (Industrial).

Twin City KTI.

Experimental track-equipped KT.

130

LINK TRACTOR

Twin City Link Tractor.

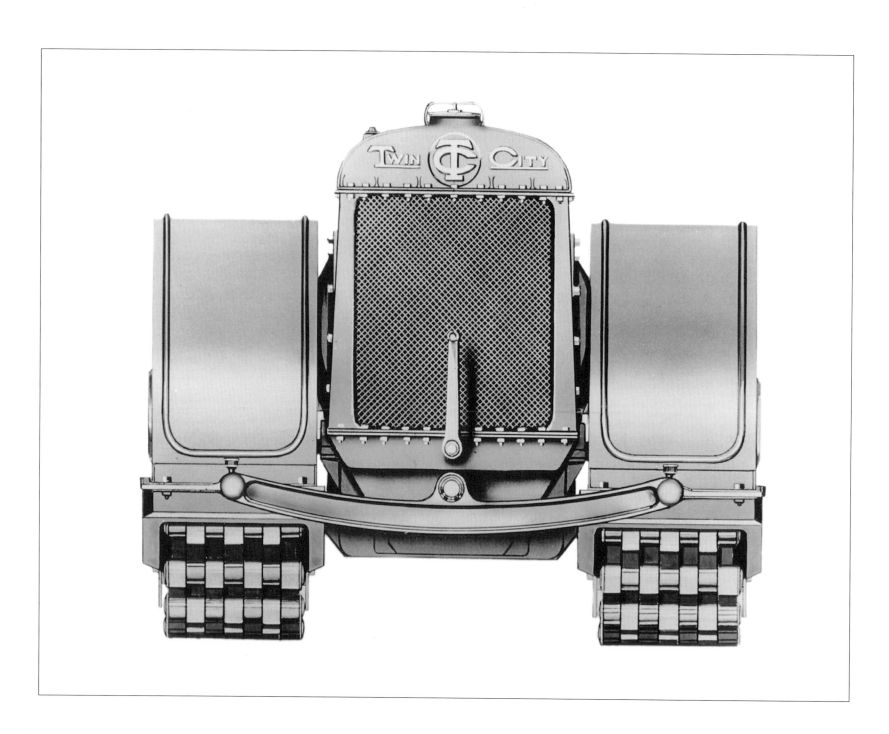

134

TWIN CITY EXPORT SHIPMENTS

Twin City service truck. Cairo, Egypt. March 1927

Photo received from Australia. July 1925.

A 12-20 being readied for export. January 1920.

Tractors on flatcars ready for transport.

Trainload of 17-28s leaving Spenser Street Station, Melbourne, Australia, to points north in Victoria.

Former President Theodore Roosevelt, during plant visit. September 1917.

The Iconografix Photo Archive Series includes:

JOHN DEERE MODEL D Photo Archive	ISBN 1-882256-00-X
JOHN DEERE MODEL B Photo Archive	ISBN 1-882256-01-8
FARMALL F-SERIES Photo Archive	ISBN 1-882256-02-6
FARMALL MODEL H Photo Archive	ISBN 1-882256-03-4
CATERPILLAR THIRTY Photo Archive	ISBN 1-882256-04-2
CATERPILLAR SIXTY Photo Archive	ISBN 1-882256-05-0
TWIN CITY TRACTOR Photo Archive	ISBN 1-882256-06-9
MINNEAPOLIS-MOLINE U-SERIES Photo Archive	ISBN 1-882256-07-7
HART-PARR Photo Archive	ISBN 1-882256-08-5
Available October 1993	
OLIVER TRACTOR Photo Archive	ISBN 1-882256-09-3
Available October 1993	

The Iconografix Photo Archive Series is available from direct mail specialty book dealers and bookstores throughout the world, or can be ordered from the publisher.
For information write to:

Iconografix
P.O. Box 609
Osceola, Wisconsin 54020

or

Telephone/Fax:
(800) 289-3504 (US and Canada only)
(715) 294-2792